W9-CYG-446

HOCKEY
RECORD BREAKERS

by Jess Myers

SportsZone
An Imprint of Abdo Publishing | abdopublishing.com

abdopublishing.com

Published by Abdo Publishing, a division of ABDO, PO Box 398166, Minneapolis, Minnesota 55439. Copyright © 2016 by Abdo Consulting Group, Inc. International copyrights reserved in all countries. No part of this book may be reproduced in any form without written permission from the publisher. SportsZone™ is a trademark and logo of Abdo Publishing.

Printed in the United States of America, North Mankato, Minnesota
042015
092015

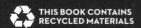

Cover Photos: Cal Sport Media/AP Images (left); Fred Jewell/AP Images (right)
Interior Photos: Cal Sport Media/AP Images, 1 (left); Fred Jewell/AP Images, 1 (right); Dave Buston/AP Images, 5; Jason Szenes/UPI Photo Service/Newscom, 7; Rusty Kennedy/AP Images, 8; Eric Draper/AP Images, 10; AP Images, 13, 14; fhj/AP Images, 16; Bill Kostroun/AP Images, 19, 20, 22; Jim Mone/AP Images, 25; Paul Hurschmann/AP Images, 27; Alex Brandon/AP Images, 28; B. Bennett/Getty Images, 31; Tony Biegun/Getty Images, 32; Mark J. Terrill/AP Images, 34; Tom Pidgeon/AP Images, 37, 42; Harold Jenkins/AP Images, 38; Carlos Osorio/AP Images, 40; Tim Shaffer/Reuters/Newscom, 44; Richard Drew/AP Images, 45

Editor: Patrick Donnelly
Series Designer: Nikki Farinella

Library of Congress Control Number: 2015931747

Cataloging-in-Publication Data
Myers, Jess.
 Hockey record breakers / Jess Myers.
   p. cm. -- (Record breakers)
Includes bibliographical references and index.
ISBN 978-1-62403-848-8
1. Hockey--Juvenile literature. 2. Hockey--Records--Juvenile literature.
I. Title.
796.962--dc23
                                        2015931747

TABLE OF CONTENTS

Note: All records in this book are current through 2014.

1

THE
GREAT ONE

Wayne Gretzky skated toward the Vancouver Canucks net. His Los Angeles Kings teammate, Marty McSorley, also closed in on Canucks goalie Kirk McLean. McSorley whipped the puck across the ice, then watched Wayne Gretzky make history.

Gretzky was known as "The Great One," and on that night in 1994 he scored his 802nd career goal. That was more than any other player in National Hockey League (NHL) history. By the time he retired, Gretzky held more than 60 NHL records.

Wayne Gretzky holds up the puck he used to score a goal for his 1,851st career point, setting an NHL record, on October 15, 1989.

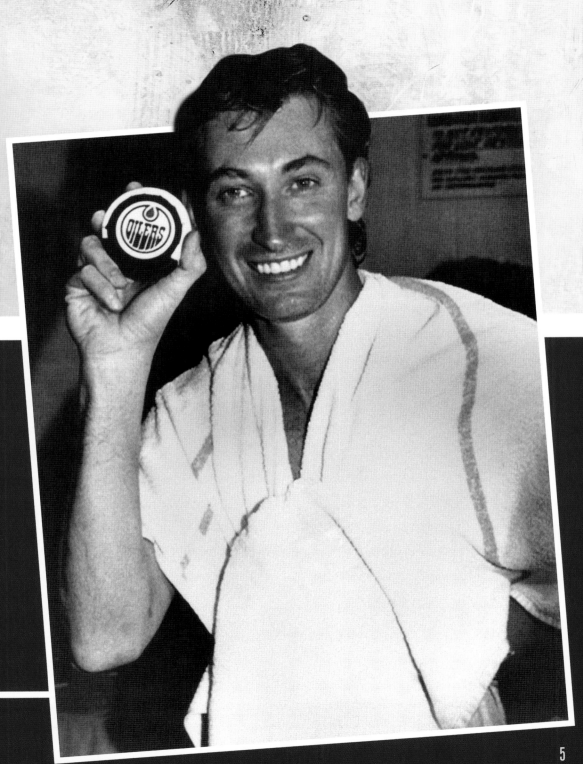

Walter and Phyllis Gretzky were living in the Canadian town of Brantford, Ontario, in the winter of 1961. Their first child—a boy they named Wayne—was born that January. From an early age, Wayne loved to skate. He played hockey on an outdoor ice rink that his father made for the family each winter.

As a teenager, Wayne became well-known throughout Canada for his hockey skills. At age 17 he started his professional career with the Indianapolis Racers of the World Hockey Association (WHA). But after only eight games, the Racers traded him to the Edmonton Oilers. In Edmonton, Gretzky became a star.

In the nearly 1,500 games he played over the course of his WHA and NHL career, Gretzky scored 894 goals and added 1,963 assists. Those are both career records. In the 1981–82 season Gretzky scored 92 goals in just 80 games. That is a record that no player has come close to breaking.

Before Gretzky arrived in the NHL, scoring 50 goals in 50 games was a remarkable feat that only a few had accomplished. In that 1981–82 season, Gretzky scored 50 goals in 39 games, setting a standard that has gone unmatched.

Gretzky did not look like a classic hockey player. He was not big or particularly fast. Instead he excelled by doing things differently. For example, hockey teams used

Wayne Gretzky celebrates after scoring a goal for the New York Rangers in the 1997 Stanley Cup Playoffs.

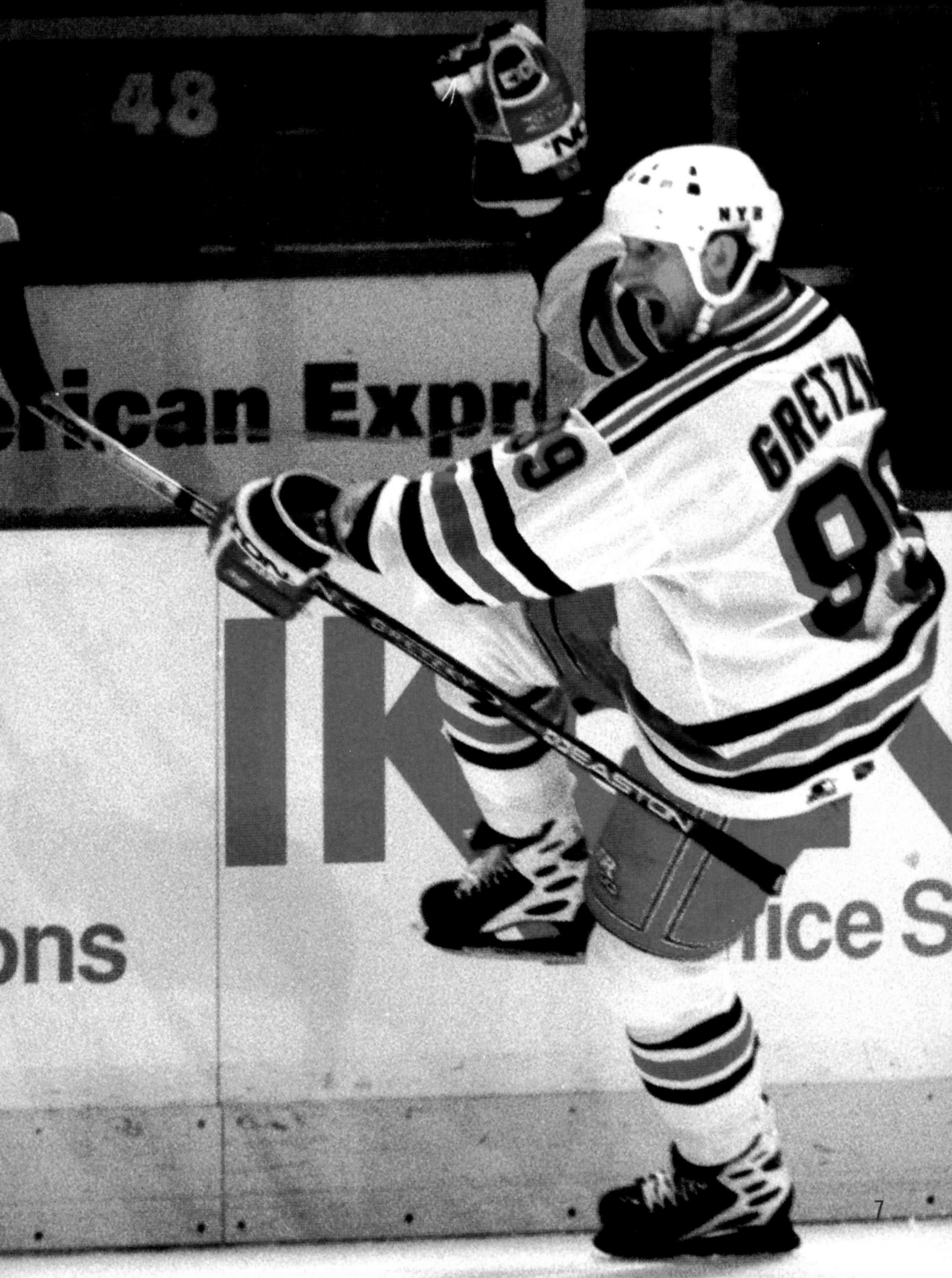
48
NYR
99
EASTON

to have 20 players who wore jerseys numbered 1 through 20. As a youth hockey player, Gretzky was so small that when he tucked his number 9 jersey into his hockey pants, it was hard to see the number. So he switched to wearing number 99.

Gretzky also used areas of the hockey rink that not many others had explored. For example, instead of always trying to pass the puck in front of the opposing goalie, Gretzky sometimes liked to hold the puck behind the net. Then the goalie had to turn around to see him. That allowed Gretzky's teammates to slip into open spots and create scoring opportunities.

Over the course of his career, Gretzky played for the Racers, Oilers, Los Angeles Kings, St. Louis Blues, and New York Rangers. His teams advanced to the playoffs in each of his first 15 professional seasons. When the playoffs began, Gretzky did some of his best work. He led all players in playoff scoring six times, including each of the four years in which his teams won the Stanley Cup.

Gretzky once joked that he believed the puck belonged to him. He would put it past the other team's goaltender quite often. But as good as he was at scoring, he may have been even better at helping others score. In the 1988 playoffs he added another record with 31 assists in just 19 games. Hockey experts say that Gretzky not only had the

Wayne Gretzky hoists the Stanley Cup after his Edmonton Oilers defeated the Boston Bruins in 1988.

Wayne Gretzky, *99*, fires the puck into the Vancouver Canucks net on March 23, 1994. His 802nd career goal set an NHL record.

ability to skate and shoot, but that he could also see plays developing. He could tell where his teammates would be, and he got them the puck before opponents saw it coming.

Gretzky retired from playing hockey in 1999. Along the way he led the NHL in scoring 11 times, including eight straight seasons (1979–80 to 1986–87). He topped the league in assists 16 times, including a 13-year streak that will be hard to beat. And his 50 career hat tricks are 10 more than the next closest player. "The Great One" truly earned his nickname in every way possible.

GORDIE HOWE: MR. HOCKEY

GORDIE HOWE WAS ONE OF THE FIRST TRUE SUPERSTARS OF HOCKEY. HE BEGAN PLAYING FOR THE DETROIT RED WINGS IN 1946 AND FINALLY HUNG UP HIS SKATES IN 1980, WHEN HE PLAYED FOR THE HARTFORD WHALERS. IN BETWEEN, HE HELPED GIVE THE UPSTART WHA A BOOST WHEN HE SIGNED WITH THE HOUSTON AEROS IN 1973. IN HOUSTON AND AGAIN IN HARTFORD HE PLAYED ALONGSIDE HIS SONS, MARK AND MARTY.

HOWE WAS ABLE TO USE HIS LEFT AND RIGHT HANDS WITH EQUAL SKILL. THAT GAVE HIM A GREAT ADVANTAGE ON THE ICE. HE COLLECTED 2,358 POINTS OVER THE COURSE OF HIS NHL AND WHA CAREER, WHICH WAS A RECORD AT THE TIME OF HIS RETIREMENT. HE HELPED THE RED WINGS WIN FOUR STANLEY CUPS AND WAS WIDELY KNOWN AS "MR. HOCKEY" BY FANS OF THE GAME EVERYWHERE.

2

THE POCKET
ROCKET

Henri Richard was used to playing in the shadow of his older brother. Maurice Richard was 14 years old when Henri was born. Maurice would go on to become a renowned goal scorer for his hometown team, the Montreal Canadiens. He remains beloved by fans across Canada as one of the most exciting players in hockey history. But Henri was the Richard brother who set a record by winning the most championships of any NHL player.

Henri Richard hugs the Stanley Cup after his overtime goal gave the Montreal Canadiens a series-clinching 3–2 win over the Detroit Red Wings in Game 6 of the 1966 Stanley Cup Finals.

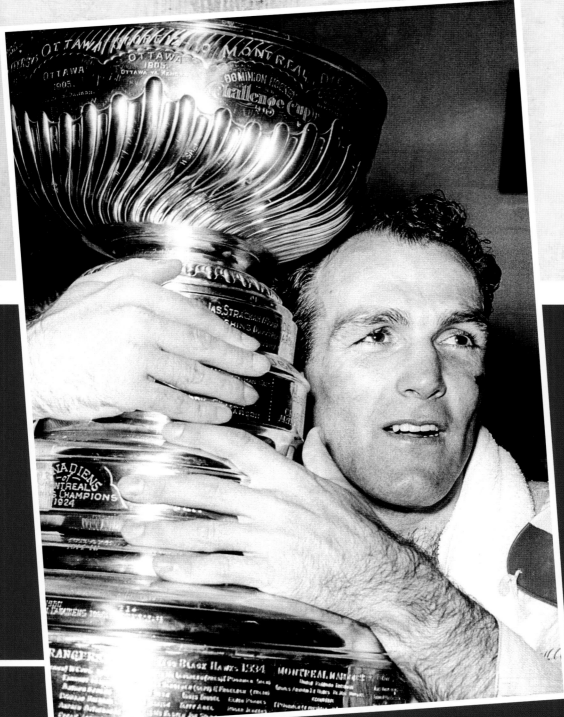

13

Maurice earned the nickname "The Rocket" for his speed and scoring ability. Henri was much younger and shorter than his brother, so when Henri also joined the Canadiens, fans nicknamed him "The Pocket Rocket." He was a skilled player and a member of many great teams in Montreal. By the time Henri retired in 1975, he had won the Stanley Cup a record 11 times.

The Stanley Cup is a huge silver trophy. The name of each player who wins it is engraved on the side of the trophy. That means "Henri Richard" is engraved into the silver in 11 different places.

Henri overcame many obstacles to become a star player. For starters, he had to live up to the family reputation established by his more popular and more famous older brother. Also, growing up in French-speaking Montreal, Henri did not speak or read much English. He eventually mastered both languages, mostly so he could speak to fans and the media in English-speaking cities in the NHL. Also, Henri stood just 5 feet 7 inches tall, making him one of the shorter players ever to star in the NHL. But Henri made up for his size with unmatched skills and hard work, which allowed him to play 20 seasons in the NHL.

Henri joined the Canadiens in 1955, when Maurice was still one of the biggest names in the NHL. At the time, some fans thought adding the younger Richard to the roster

Henri Richard, *center*, fights through a scrum against the Boston Bruins in a 1958 game.

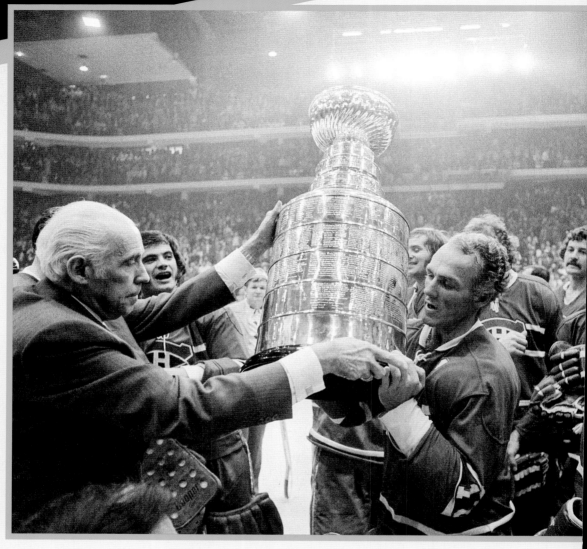

NHL president Clarence Campbell, *left*, hands the Stanley Cup to Canadiens captain Henri Richard after Montreal defeated Chicago in the 1973 Stanley Cup Finals.

was little more than a publicity stunt. But the Canadiens won the Stanley Cup that year, starting a six-year streak as NHL champions.

Henri's last Stanley Cup championship came in the 1972–73 season, when Montreal beat the Chicago

Blackhawks in the Finals. By the time he retired, Henri had played 1,256 games for Montreal, which is a team record.

Henri wore the number 16 jersey throughout his career. The Canadiens retired that number, meaning no player for Montreal will ever wear it again. He was elected to the Hockey Hall of Fame in 1979.

SCOTTY BOWMAN: COACHING LEGEND

WHEREVER SCOTTY BOWMAN COACHED, THE STANLEY CUP SEEMED TO FOLLOW HIM. BOWMAN STARTED HIS NHL COACHING CAREER WITH THE ST. LOUIS BLUES IN 1967. HE THEN MOVED TO CANADA TO COACH THE MONTREAL CANADIENS IN 1971. HE LED THE CANADIENS TO THE PLAYOFFS EIGHT TIMES IN THE EIGHT YEARS HE COACHED THEM. THEY WON THE STANLEY CUP FIVE TIMES IN THAT STRETCH.

LATER IN HIS COACHING CAREER, BOWMAN KEPT WINNING. HE GUIDED THE PITTSBURGH PENGUINS TO THE STANLEY CUP IN 1992. THEN HE COACHED THE DETROIT RED WINGS TO STANLEY CUP VICTORIES IN 1997, 1998, AND 2002. HIS NINE STANLEY CUP WINS AS A COACH ARE THE MOST IN NHL HISTORY.

3

MARTY STOPS THEM ALL

As a boy growing up in Montreal, Martin Brodeur was no stranger to NHL hockey. His father, Denis, had been a pretty good hockey player himself. Denis played for Canada in the 1956 Winter Olympics. When Martin was growing up, Denis was the official team photographer for the Montreal Canadiens. So young Martin would spend lots of time following his father to practices and to games at the legendary Montreal Forum.

Martin Brodeur celebrates after he helped the New Jersey Devils sweep the 1995 Stanley Cup Finals.

Martin Brodeur stops a shot by Alexei Kovalev of the New York Rangers during the 1994 Stanley Cup playoffs.

In the late 1980s and early 1990s, the Canadiens had a great young goaltender named Patrick Roy. In 1986 and again in 1993, Roy helped the Canadiens win the Stanley Cup. Roy was Brodeur's idol, and he was one of the reasons that Brodeur chose to switch to playing goalie after playing forward for a time as a youth hockey player.

And when he played goalie, Brodeur was good at it. He was so good that the New Jersey Devils picked him in the first round of the NHL draft in 1990. The Devils had never been a very competitive team. But the arrival of Brodeur in goal and a new coach behind the bench changed things in a hurry.

In the 1993–94 season, Brodeur had a great rookie year in goal. It helped that Jacques Lemaire coached the Devils to play a defense-first system. That limited their opponents' scoring chances. The Devils made a run in the playoffs and nearly made it to the Stanley Cup Finals. With 27 wins that season, Brodeur was named the best rookie in the NHL.

One year later, Brodeur won 19 games in a regular season that was shortened because of a labor dispute. Then he won 16 more in the playoffs as the Devils brought the Stanley Cup to New Jersey for the first time. They knocked off the heavily favored Detroit Red Wings to do so, and Brodeur was in goal for all of the Devils' playoff victories.

In all, Brodeur would spend 20 full seasons with the Devils, rarely taking a night off. In a hockey season that lasts 82 games, Brodeur would often play 70 or more games per season. Being New Jersey's backup goaltender could get pretty boring.

Brodeur's work in goal helped the Devils win the Stanley Cup again in 2000 and 2003. In 2001 and 2012 they fell just short, losing in the Stanley Cup Finals. Brodeur also followed in his father's path and played for his country on several occasions. He skated for Team Canada at the

Martin Brodeur displays the form that helped him set the record for most victories and shutouts by an NHL goaltender.

Olympics three times, and he helped Canada win the gold medal in 2002 and again in 2010.

In the 2008–09 season, Brodeur surpassed his idol, breaking Roy's record of 551 career victories. He also holds the record for most shutouts in an NHL career. At the end of the 2013–14 season, Brodeur had 688 wins, all with the Devils. He then signed with the St. Louis Blues in November 2014 and won three more games before finally retiring with 691 career victories and 125 shutouts.

PATRICK ROY: STANLEY CUP STALWART

NHL HOCKEY IS AN INTENSE GAME, BUT THE PRESSURE RISES IN THE PLAYOFFS. NO PRO GOALIE KNOWS THIS BETTER THAN PATRICK ROY, WHO RETIRED IN 2003 AS THE NHL'S ALL-TIME LEADER IN PLAYOFF WINS. ROY BEGAN HIS HOCKEY CAREER WITH THE MONTREAL CANADIENS. HE HELPED MONTREAL WIN THE STANLEY CUP IN 1986 AND AGAIN IN 1993, AND HE WAS NAMED THE PLAYOFFS MOST VALUABLE PLAYER (MVP) BOTH TIMES.

IN DECEMBER 1995, ROY WAS TRADED TO THE COLORADO AVALANCHE, WHO WERE PLAYING THEIR FIRST SEASON IN DENVER. LATER THAT SEASON, WITH ROY IN GOAL, THE AVALANCHE WON THE STANLEY CUP. IN 2001 ROY HELPED THE AVALANCHE WIN THE STANLEY CUP A SECOND TIME. HE RETIRED WITH AN NHL RECORD 151 PLAYOFF WINS. BRODEUR IS THE ONLY OTHER GOALIE WITH MORE THAN 92 CAREER POSTSEASON VICTORIES.

4
PENGUINS
CAN FLY

B y March 1993 it had already been a tough season for the Pittsburgh Penguins. They had won the Stanley Cup in each of the previous two seasons, and fans in western Pennsylvania were wild about their team. For years they had packed the domed arena in downtown Pittsburgh that had been nicknamed "the Igloo." But the Penguins had some challenges.

Pittsburgh Penguins captain Mario Lemieux hoists the Stanley Cup in 1991. Two years later he would return from a serious illness to help the Penguins set an NHL record for consecutive victories.

They had lost seven of their previous 10 games. And their best player, widely considered the best player in all of hockey, was ill. Mario Lemieux, a towering goal scorer and former NHL MVP, had been feeling sick for months. Earlier that season he had learned he suffered from Hodgkin's Disease, which is a form of cancer. It was not life threatening, but it kept him off the ice for part of the season.

But on March 9, Lemieux returned to the Igloo to play his first home game since he had been diagnosed with the disease. The Penguins won that night, beating the Boston Bruins 3–2. Two nights later, the Penguins beat the Los Angeles Kings 4–3 in overtime when Jaromir Jagr scored a power-play goal. Soon the Penguins could not lose.

They won a road game against the New York Islanders. Then they came back to Pittsburgh for consecutive home games versus the Washington Capitals and Philadelphia Flyers and won both. They beat the Edmonton Oilers 6–4 in a neutral-site game in Cleveland, Ohio. Then they beat the San Jose Sharks and New Jersey Devils back at home.

The Penguins kept winning every game they played for more than a month. They clinched the President's Trophy, which is given each year to the team with the best regular-season record in the NHL. On April 7, the Penguins had a home game versus the Montreal Canadiens. Pittsburgh had

Mario Lemieux, *left*, fires a shot on goal as Travis Green of the New York Islanders looks on in a 1993 Stanley Cup playoff game.

Mario Lemieux, *left*, looks dejected as four New York Islanders celebrate their Game 6 victory in the second round of the Stanley Cup playoffs. The Islanders shocked the Penguins in Game 7, ending Pittsburgh's quest for three straight titles.

won 14 straight, needing one more to tie the NHL record for consecutive wins, which was then held by the 1982 Islanders. Ulf Samuelsson scored in overtime, giving the Penguins a share of the record.

A few nights later they traveled to Madison Square Garden in the heart of New York City and claimed the record for themselves in a big way. Lemieux scored an amazing five goals as the Penguins beat the New York Rangers 10–4. The next night they beat the Rangers again, this time in Pittsburgh, 4–2 for their seventeenth win in a row. It is a record that still stands today.

The Penguins skated to a 6–6 tie with the New Jersey Devils in their final regular-season game that year, bringing the streak to a halt. They had won 17 straight games and had outscored their opponents 96–48 in the process. However, the Penguins could not keep their momentum going. They were a heavy favorite to win a third straight Stanley Cup. But the Islanders upset them in the second round of the playoffs.

They would not win another NHL championship with Lemieux skating for the team. But they set a mark for consecutive victories that will be tough to beat.

FLOUNDERING SHARKS

WHILE THINGS WERE GOING WELL FOR PITTSBURGH THAT SEASON, IT WAS A DIFFERENT STORY ON THE OTHER SIDE OF THE COUNTRY. OUT IN CALIFORNIA, THE SAN JOSE SHARKS WERE PLAYING JUST THEIR SECOND SEASON IN THE NHL. THEY PLAYED THEIR HOME GAMES NOT IN SAN JOSE BUT SEVERAL MILES AWAY IN SAN FRANCISCO, WHILE THEIR NEW ARENA WAS BEING BUILT. THEIR TEMPORARY HOME ARENA, NAMED THE COW PALACE, DID NOT SOUND MUCH LIKE A HOCKEY RINK. AND THAT SEASON, THE SHARKS WERE NOT A VERY SUCCESSFUL HOCKEY TEAM.

ON JANUARY 4, 1993, THE SHARKS LOST TO THE MONTREAL CANADIENS. THEY WOULD GO ON TO LOSE ANOTHER 16 IN A ROW BEFORE FINALLY WINNING ON VALENTINE'S DAY. SAN JOSE'S 3–2 WIN OVER THE WINNIPEG JETS SNAPPED A 17-GAME LOSING STREAK. TO THIS DAY, NO NHL TEAM HAS EVER LOST MORE THAN 17 GAMES IN A ROW.

5

TEEMU'S AMAZING DEBUT

Everyone wants to make a good first impression. In the 1992–93 season, Teemu Selanne made the most notable first impression of any rookie in NHL history. Selanne was already a successful and talented hockey player in Finland, his home country. There he had attended business school, taught kindergarten part-time, and served in the Finnish military. He also scored a lot of goals for a team named Jokerit. After skating for his country in the 1992 Winter Olympics, Selanne helped Jokerit win the Finnish league championship.

Teemu Selanne broke into the NHL in the 1992–93 season with a dynamite rookie season for the Winnipeg Jets.

At age 22, Selanne decided it was time for a new challenge. The Winnipeg Jets had selected him in the first round of the 1988 NHL draft. Four years later, he came to the largest city in Manitoba to see if he could match his European success on the rinks of North America.

Selanne had two assists in his first NHL game. In his second game, he scored a goal. In his fifth game, Selanne scored a hat trick. After playing 12 games in the NHL, he already had 11 goals and was suddenly the talk of the NHL. Selanne quickly earned the nickname "the Finnish Flash." He also became known for his unique celebration after scoring a goal. Selanne would hold his stick like a shotgun and "fire" into the air like a hunter shooting at a bird. Fans began packing arenas when the Jets would come to town. They all wanted to see this scoring wonder.

In 1978 Mike Bossy of the New York Islanders had set the NHL record for goals by a first-year player with 53. In early 1993, Selanne scored his 40th goal with 32 games remaining. Talk began to swirl that Bossy's record might be in danger.

On March 2, 1993, Selanne notched a hat trick against the Quebec Nordiques, giving him 54 goals on the season. With more than a month left in the regular season, Selanne was far from finished. An assist on March 23 gave Selanne 110 points, breaking the NHL record for rookies. That was

Teemu Selanne of the Winnipeg Jets shows off his unique celebration after his record-breaking goal on March 2, 1993.

Teemu Selanne, shown here in 1997, went on to win a Stanley Cup with the Anaheim Ducks in 2007.

previously held by another European star, Peter Stastny of the Nordiques.

The Jets' last regular season game that year was at home against the Edmonton Oilers. As he had done so many other times that season, Selanne scored one of his team's goals in a 3–0 Jets win. That gave him 76 goals on the season, a rookie record that still stands today. In fact, only four players have ever scored more in one year.

Selanne tied with Buffalo's Alexander Mogilny for the NHL lead in goals that season. He was an easy pick for the NHL's Rookie of the Year Award. He would go on to play a total of 21 seasons in the NHL before retiring in 2014. Selanne scored 684 goals in his career, but he never again came close to matching the 76 that he scored in that first magical season in Winnipeg. His next-best total was 52 goals in the 1997–98 season.

AL HILL: ONE-HIT WONDER

OVER THE COURSE OF HIS CAREER, AL HILL PLAYED IN 221 GAMES FOR THE PHILADELPHIA FLYERS. BUT NONE OF THOSE GAMES WAS AS GOOD AS HIS FIRST ONE. ON FEBRUARY 14, 1977, HILL MADE HIS NHL DEBUT FOR THE FLYERS IN A HOME GAME VERSUS THE ST. LOUIS BLUES.

PHILADELPHIA WON THE GAME 6–4, THANKS IN LARGE PART TO HILL. THE ROOKIE SCORED TWO GOALS AND ADDED THREE ASSISTS. HILL'S FIVE POINTS IN HIS FIRST-EVER NHL GAME STILL STANDS AS A LEAGUE RECORD FOR A DEBUT.

6

RED WINGS
TAKE FLIGHT

The city of Detroit was thriving in the 1950s. The American automobile industry was at its peak. Jobs were plentiful in Michigan's largest city, which was nicknamed "The Motor City." And that success was reflected on the ice as well, as the Detroit Red Wings were Stanley Cup champions four times in the decade.

Detroit's Paul Coffey, *left*, congratulates goalie Mike Vernon after a 7–0 win over the Colorado Avalanche clinched the second straight President's Trophy for the Red Wings in 1996.

By the 1980s, the city and its hockey team had fallen on tough times. Jobs were hard to come by as automobile plants closed or downsized. On the ice, the Red Wings struggled, earning the nickname "Dead Wings" from many disappointed fans.

But the 1990s brought a turnaround for Detroit hockey. With a cast of talented young stars playing at Joe Louis Arena, the Red Wings finally made it back to the Stanley Cup Finals in 1995. They lost to the upstart New Jersey Devils, but the playoff run was sign that good times were on the horizon.

Everything seemed to click for the Red Wings in the next regular season. In 1995–96 the Red Wings set a record that still stands today by winning 62 out of 82 regular-season games. No other team that season won more than 49 games.

Detroit built its roster around star forward Steve Yzerman, whom they drafted fourth overall in 1983. Then along came Sergei Fedorov, a young star from Russia who had left the Soviet Union in 1990 to play for the Red Wings. Fedorov was soon joined by several of his countrymen: defensemen Slava Fetisov and Vladimir Konstantinov, along with forwards Igor Larionov and Slava Kozlov. The four men had played on the same professional team in Moscow.

Detroit Red Wings forward Kris Draper celebrates scoring a short-handed goal against the St. Louis Blues in a 1996 Stanley Cup playoff game.

Detroit Red Wings goalie Chris Osgood makes a save against the St. Louis Blues in a 1996 Stanley Cup playoff game.

Together, along with Fedorov, they earned the nickname "The Russian Five."

The Detroit coach was a man who knew a thing or two about winning as well. Scotty Bowman had won five Stanley Cups while coaching the Montreal Canadiens in the 1970s. He then led the Pittsburgh Penguins to the Stanley Cup in 1991–92. Bowman left Pittsburgh to take over behind the Detroit bench in 1993. He would eventually win three Cups with the Red Wings, but 1995–96 was by far his best regular season. Between November 25 and January 3 that season, Detroit lost just once. The Red Wings easily captured the President's Trophy, which is given to the NHL's top regular-season team.

Interestingly, before all of those wins, Detroit's first game of the season was a loss to the Colorado Avalanche. And its record-setting season would end the same way.

The Red Wings opened the playoffs versus the Winnipeg Jets, who would be moving to Arizona at the end of the season. Detroit won an emotional six-game series, beating Winnipeg 4-1 in Game 6, which was the final game played by the Jets at Winnipeg Arena.

The second round exhibited more dramatic hockey, as the St. Louis Blues—who featured the great Wayne Gretzky at the time—pushed the Red Wings to their absolute limit. Trailing three games to two in the series, the Red Wings went to St. Louis and beat the Blues in Game 6, then came home to Detroit for a hard-fought final game. Gretzky and Yzerman seemingly never left the ice in Game 7. And goalies Jon Casey of the Blues and Chris Osgood of the Red

41

Detroit Red Wings center Steve Yzerman, *front*, skates behind the net shadowed by St. Louis Blues defenseman Igor Kravchuk during the 1996 Stanley Cup playoffs.

Wings blocked every shot that came their way in all three periods, and in the first overtime.

Yzerman finally ended it in the second extra session. He grabbed a puck that had bounced off Gretzky's stick, raced toward the St. Louis net, and blasted a slap shot from near the blue line. The puck slipped past Casey, and the Red Wings had a 1–0 victory in double overtime to advance to round three.

But after their remarkable regular season and two emotional and exhausting playoff series, the Red Wings had little gas left in the tank. The Avalanche—who had the second-best record in the NHL that season—pulled off the upset in six games. The Red Wings had made history in 1995–96, but they fell short in their quest to bring the Stanley Cup back to Detroit.

CAPITAL PUNISHMENT

THE WASHINGTON CAPITALS JOINED THE NHL AS AN EXPANSION TEAM IN 1974. AND AS FIRST-YEAR TEAMS SO OFTEN DO, THE CAPITALS STRUGGLED. THEY WERE OUTSCORED 12–3 IN THEIR FIRST TWO GAMES, BOTH LOPSIDED LOSSES ON THE ROAD. THE CAPS EARNED A TIE WITH THE LOS ANGELES KINGS IN THEIR FIRST-EVER HOME GAME, AND ON OCTOBER 17, 1974, THEY WON THEIR FIRST GAME, BEATING THE CHICAGO BLACKHAWKS 4–3. THEY WOULD NOT WIN ANOTHER GAME FOR MORE THAN A MONTH. THEY ALMOST WENT WINLESS ON THE ROAD THE ENTIRE SEASON. THEY FINALLY BEAT THE CALIFORNIA GOLDEN SEALS 5–3 IN OAKLAND ON MARCH 28, WITH JUST TWO ROAD GAMES LEFT ON THE SCHEDULE. IN ALL, THE CAPITALS WON JUST EIGHT OF THE 80 GAMES THEY PLAYED IN 1974–75, WHICH STILL STANDS AS AN NHL RECORD FOR FEWEST WINS IN A SEASON.

FUN FACTS

PENALTIES APLENTY

When the Ottawa Senators and Philadelphia Flyers played on March 5, 2004, five penalties were called in the first two periods. But multiple fights broke out in the third period, resulting in 60 more penalties. The game stands as a record, with 419 penalty minutes assessed to the two teams.

GOALS AND MORE GOALS

On December 11, 1985, the Edmonton Oilers beat the Chicago Blackhawks 12–9, tying the NHL record for most goals by two teams in one game. Amazingly, Wayne Gretzky did not score a goal for the Oilers, but he did tie an NHL record with seven assists. Gretzky's linemates, Glenn Anderson and Jari Kurri, each recorded hat tricks.

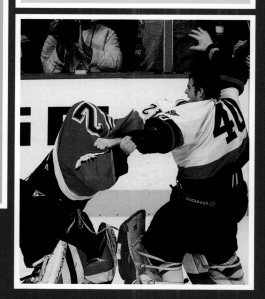

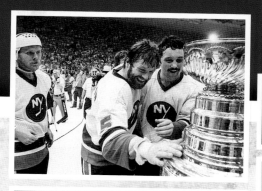

NOT A BAD WEEK

On February 24, 1980, Dave Christian won a gold medal with the US Olympic hockey team. Just five days later, Christian scored seven seconds into his first shift in an NHL game, a 3–3 tie between his Winnipeg Jets and the Vancouver Canucks. That remains a record for the fastest goal to start an NHL career.

PLAYOFFS ON THE ISLAND

The New York Islanders struggled when they entered the NHL in 1972, but they soon were a powerhouse. Between 1980 and 1984, the Islanders won four Stanley Cups and 19 consecutive playoff series, which stands as an NHL record.

GLOSSARY

assist
A pass to a teammate that leads to a goal.

expansion
When a league grows by adding a new team or teams.

hat trick
When a player scores three goals in a game.

linemates
A trio of forwards—left wing, center, and right wing—who usually play at the same time.

overtime
The time added to the end of a game if no winner is decided during regulation time.

power play
When a team has more players on the ice than the opponent because of the opponent's penalties.

puck
A hard, black rubber disk used in hockey rather than a ball.

shutout
When a goaltender plays an entire game without the other team scoring a goal.

FOR MORE INFORMATION

Graves, Will. *The Best Hockey Players of All Time*. Minneapolis, MN: Abdo Publishing, 2015.

Peters, Chris. *Stanley Cup Finals*. Minneapolis, MN: Abdo Publishing, 2013.

Zweig, Eric. *Super Scorers*. Richmond Hill, Ontario, Canada: Firefly Books, 2014.

WEBSITES

To learn more about Record Breakers, visit **booklinks.abdopublishing.com**. These links are routinely monitored and updated to provide the most current information available.

PLACE TO VISIT

Hockey Hall of Fame
30 Yonge Street
Toronto, Ontario M5E 1X8
Canada
(416) 360-7765
www.hhof.com
This hall of fame celebrates the history of hockey and its greatest players and contributors through memorabilia and other interactive exhibits. Among the highlights of the museum is the opportunity to view the original Stanley Cup trophy.

INDEX

ABOUT THE AUTHOR

Jess Myers was raised in the small town of Warroad, Minnesota, which is known by many as "Hockeytown USA." His first youth hockey coach was an Olympic gold medal winner. He and his wife live outside St. Paul, Minnesota, with three children who all play hockey.